CUTTING-EDGE TECHNOLOGY

GMOs

Mary Colson

Gareth Stevens
PUBLISHING

Please visit our website, **www.garethstevens.com**.
For a free color catalog of all our high-quality books,
call toll free 1-800-542-2595 or fax 1-877-542-2596.

Cataloging-in-Publication Data
Names: Colson, Mary.
Title: GMOs / Mary Colson.
Description: New York : Gareth Stevens Publishing, 2017. | Series: Cutting-edge technology | Includes index.
Identifiers: ISBN 9781482451634 (pbk.) | ISBN 9781482451573 (library bound) | ISBN 9781482451450 (6 pack)
Subjects: LCSH: Genetically modified foods–Juvenile literature.
Classification: LCC TP248.65.F66 C65 2017 | DDC 641.3–dc23

First Edition

Published in 2017 by
Gareth Stevens Publishing
111 East 14th Street, Suite 349
New York, NY 10003

© 2017 Gareth Stevens Publishing

Produced for Gareth Stevens by Calcium
Editors: Sarah Eason and Harriet McGregor
Designer: Simon Borrough
Picture researcher: Rachel Blount

Picture credits: Cover: Getty Images: Zomi (photo), Shutterstock: Eky Studio (banner), Shutterstock: R-studio (back cover bkgrd); Inside: Shutterstock: 06photo 16, Angellodeco 35, Mikkel Bigandt 23, Featureflash 24, Szasz-Fabian Jozsef 8, Kalewa 27, Oleksiy Mark 7, Miroslav K 30, Natursports 33, Palenque 42, Pedrosala 5, Promotive 41, Cheryl Ann Quigley 13, Zeljko Radojko 11, Pete Saloutos 37, Nick Starichenko 15, talseN 21, Vlad Teodor 45, Vivid Pixels 28; Utah State University: Lewis Spider Silk Laboratory 39; Wikimedia Commons: www.glofish.com 1, 19.

Printed in the United States of America
CPSIA compliance information: Batch #CS16GS: For further information contact Gareth Stevens, New York, New York at 1-800-542-2595.

CONTENTS

Chapter 1	GMOs	4
Chapter 2	Creating Crops	10
Chapter 3	Altered Animals	18
Chapter 4	Making Medicine	24
Chapter 5	Cloning	30
Chapter 6	New Uses for GMOs	38
Glossary		46
For More Information		47
Index		48

GMOs

In laboratories all over the world, scientists are experimenting with the microscopic, or very tiny, chemical building blocks of life itself, called **genes**. By using, mixing, and changing genes, scientists have already created fish that glow in the dark, plants that can kill their own pests, and farm animals that produce more milk or meat. The technology could mean the future of the human race will be modified too.

WHAT ARE GMOS?

Genetically modified organisms (GMOs) are what we call plants and animals that have been genetically altered by scientists. They exist in many areas of our daily lives, from pets and food to medicine and agriculture. If we modify or change genes, we can create new species, make crops pest-resistant, and in some cases even cure diseases. In time, genetic modification (GM) might also save lives. But what is the catch? Is it all too good to be true?

USES OF GM

GM is one of a number of new sciences called **biotechnology**. This branch of science allows scientists to put living things to new uses, such as producing new medicines. GM changes the genes and therefore the characteristics of a plant or an animal. It makes it possible to transfer genes from one species to another. When scientists genetically modify a plant, they insert a foreign gene into the plant's own genes. This might be a gene from an organism that is resistant to pesticide. The plant adds the new gene to its own **genetic code** and also becomes pesticide-resistant.

CUTTING EDGE

The latest must-have GM animal is a glittery gold sea horse. Scientists in Vietnam mixed gold dust with jellyfish proteins. This was then inserted into sea horse eggs using the cutting-edge "gene shooting method." For more on how this method might be used for treating currently incurable human diseases, see page 28.

Genetically modified foods are first grown under carefully controlled conditions in a laboratory. Scientists monitor the plants' development closely.

This book looks at GMOs and assesses how they can benefit our lives. It also explores some of the devastating side effects of tampering with nature.

All life on Earth, from tiny microscopic **bacteria** and plants to humans and blue whales, has genes. A gene is a code that governs how a life form appears, develops, grows, and what characteristics it has. Genes will decide what color a flower is or how tall a plant can grow.

WHAT IS IN A CELL?

A cell is the basic structural unit of all living things. It holds the biological information to keep an organism alive. Living things can have one cell, like bacteria, or they can have many billions, like humans. Each different type of cell has a different purpose. For example, some of the cells in the human body control the nerves while others control eye color. A human body has more than 200 different types of cell, all doing a different job to help the body function. There are blood cells, bone cells, and cells that make up muscles.

INHERITED FEATURES

The **nucleus** is the control center of a cell. Here, all of an organism's genetic information is stored. Humans get half of their genes from their mothers and half from their fathers. Genes make animals look like their parents, so a human child

GENETICS GENIUS

Gregor Mendel (1822–1884) was an Austrian monk who studied genetic inheritance in pea plants in his monastery garden. He grew more than 10,000 plants and studied them closely. He realized that genes come in pairs, with one gene inherited from the mother and one from the father plant. Today, Mendel is considered the "father of genetics" because his work made everything that followed in genetic science possible.

Cb =pH[H⁻]	[OH⁻]
7.40 3.98E-08	2.51E-07
7.60 2.51E-08	3.98E-07
8.00 1.00E-08	1.00E-06
8.40 3.98E-09	2.51E-06
8.80 1.58E-09	6.31E-06
9.00 1.00E-09	1.00E-05
9.40 3.98E-10	2.51E-05

This is a **deoxyribonucleic acid (DNA) molecule**. If you unravelled all the DNA molecules in your body and placed them end to end, they would stretch to the sun and back several times!

may have brown eyes like its father. A baby zebra has stripes and a leopard has spots because their parents passed on these features through their genes. Like people and animals, the characteristics of a plant will be transferred to its offspring, so oak seeds can only grow into oak trees and so on.

All genes, whether they are human, plant, animal, or bacterial are created from the same material. This material is called DNA. It is a mix of four different chemicals arranged in a variety ways to make each person, creature, and plant unique, or one-of-a-kind.

ADAPTING NATURE

Since Gregor Mendel's breakthrough in the mid-nineteenth century, the study of cell biology has caused both fascination and fear. If scientists know how the human body works, they can look for cures for all sorts of medical problems such as poor eyesight, inherited diseases, and even organ failure.

CHEMICAL CHARACTERISTICS

In 1869, Swiss physician Friedrich Miescher (1844–1895) identified a chemical that he named nuclein. Today, we call this DNA. Following this, many scientists studied the idea of inherited characteristics, both in plants and in animals. British zoologist Charles Darwin (1809–1882) proposed the theory of the survival of the fittest. This means that only the strongest individuals of any plant or animal will survive.

Mice are often used in gene experiments because their genetic makeup closely resembles that of a human's.

Genetics is a relatively young science but progress has been rapid. In 1974, the first genetically modified organism was created. By 1980, the first genetically modified mouse was created, and in 1982, the U.S. Food and Drug Administration approved the first genetically engineered medicine. This was a form of insulin, used to treat some types of diabetes.

CRACKING THE CODE OF LIFE

In 1913, American biologist Alfred Sturtevant (1891–1970) created a genetic map that looked at how genes join together in fertilization, the process in which offspring are created. From the 1920s to the 1940s, scientists all over the world were in an academic race to crack the "code of life" and to figure out the exact structure and nature of DNA.

In 1953, scientists James Watson (born 1928) and Francis Crick (1916–2004) published the results of their studies into the structure of DNA. This was a game-changing breakthrough. Three years later, American geneticist Joe Hin Tijo (1919–2001) established that humans have 46 **chromosomes**, or strings of DNA, containing all our genetic information.

THE HUMAN GENOME PROJECT

In the last 50 years, scientists have unlocked the structure and process of DNA and created a genetic map, charting all the genes in the human body. The Human Genome Project was an international research project to map all the genes of human DNA. It began in 1990 and was completed in 2003. It involved scientists from all over the world and is, so far, the world's biggest collaborative science project.

CHAPTER 2

CREATING CROPS

Changing nature and making it do what we want is what humans have been doing for thousands of years. Since the dawn of farming, people have bred the best animals and plants to get more meat and better harvests. This is called selective breeding and happens very slowly over many years. GM is the latest step in this process.

Genetically modifying crops means that they can fight off insects or disease and ensure a bigger harvest. As families have grown larger and populations have increased, the demand for food has risen. This has meant a focus on maximizing harvests and producing as much meat as possible. Population growth has also meant that more materials are required. For example, cotton has been genetically modified to protect the plant from insect damage. This will guarantee the cotton harvest for the textiles industry.

PERFECT FOOD?

Today, all over the world, many crops have been genetically modified to be cheaper, reduce waste, and ensure harvests and food supply chains continue in extreme weather. In the United States, rapeseed, soya, corn, and cotton have all been genetically modified to grow faster, yield higher, resist pests, and guarantee a harvest during the worst weather. Today, GM scientists are working on crops that may taste better. They are also working on "smart plants" that monitor their own growth.

Farmers need only spray GM crops with pesticide once. This saves the farmer money and uses fewer chemicals, which is better for the environment.

SPOT THE DIFFERENCE

From the outside, GM plants like tomatoes and wheat do not look any different from nonGM plants, and they probably do not taste any different. However, they might have an extra property, like extra vitamins or frost resistance.

THE LEFTOVERS?

Many people worry that GM food is being grown without enough testing or studies into possible long-term side effects. They think that genes from GM crops might harm the natural world or pollute our drinking water. Some scientists are also against GM food. They think that GM crops could wipe out wild plants or create superstrong weeds. A large group of people, including scientists and members of the public, think that GM crops should not be planted until we are absolutely sure that they are safe.

ENGINEERING OR BREEDING?

Over a very long time, through selective breeding, farmers can make their animals grow larger or produce more milk. This is considered a good way to farm and to produce more food. It is not a natural process, but we have come to view it as such.

Over time, selective breeding has created new species. Hill farmers have crossbred sheep by, for example, mating a tough local sheep that can withstand the cold with a thick-fleeced breed to produce a thick-fleeced, hardy breed. Pigs and cattle have also been bred selectively. Genetic engineering can speed up this process and can also do something nature and selective breeding cannot do.

BEYOND NATURE

In theory, because scientists now understand how genes and DNA work, they could take a gene from any plant or animal and add it to another to modify that plant or animal in some way. For example, they could take a gene from a fish that swims in the Arctic and add it to a plant. The fish gene would keep the fish from freezing in the icy sea and it would help the plant survive cold weather. Scale up the process to humans, and those who suffer from circulation problems could be helped in a similar way.

Through GM science, growth genes are being added to pigs, salmon, and sheep. Other genes are added to make animals with less fat and more meat. The potential for improving quality of life is huge, but there are concerns about how far science should be allowed to tamper with nature. In many countries, strict laws govern genetic modification and what scientists can and cannot do.

Racehorses have been carefully selected to retain the best specimens, called thoroughbreds. These horses can run extremely fast.

CUTTING EDGE

Very few GM animals are healthy. Many of the pigs and sheep that scientists have changed with human genes have serious illnesses. To date, transferring human genes into plants or other animals has not been very successful. Human-to-human gene transfer works, but successfully crossing the species boundary is one of the next challenges for geneticists.

HOW TO FEED THE WORLD?

By 2050, the United Nations estimates that the world's population will be 9 billion. This will have a huge impact on resources, including food supplies. Many scientists believe that GM food could help both feed a growing global population and end hunger in poorer parts of the world.

In Israel and the United States, scientists are working on GM corn that can grow in dry or cold areas. In Asia, where the main food is rice, many people lack vitamin A and lose their sight. Currently in development, GM rice has vitamin A added to it. If successful, it would provide an extra level of nutrition and perhaps lower the rate of blindness.

HOW GM CAN HELP BUSINESS

Genetically modifying food can help prolong its life, which in turn can help feed more people. For example, a lot of food rots very quickly after it is harvested. When people in hot countries export fruit overseas, they want it to ripen slowly, not bruise, and stay fresh longer. If the food lasts longer, if can travel farther and be sold to more people. Scientists have already genetically modified melons so that they ripen more slowly. Tomatoes have also been modified so that they are larger and juicier. Strawberries have been made sweeter. All these changes (and many others) can have very positive social and economic consequences for farmers and communities.

GM can help minimize the damage done to crops by insects such as this grasshopper. This would mean higher yields and a more certain food supply.

CUTTING EDGE

In North America, the corn rootworm causes a lot of damage to corn plants. Scientists found that tiny bacteria in the soil contained a chemical called Bt that kills the young rootworm. Through GM, scientists have added the Bt gene to corn plants to create a crop that makes its own pest-killer. Unfortunately, the pollen from GM corn can also kill butterflies and harm other living things.

FRANKENSTEIN FOODS?

GM food is any food that contains part of GM plants or GM animals. Many processed foods such as soups, sauces, and pastries contain GM crops. GM foods are controversial. This means that people have very different and strong opinions about them. Some people feel that GM food is an important development that will help farmers produce more food at lower costs and feed more people. Others worry that this new science will bring unknown and unexpected dangers. There is no long-term data or evidence about any possible side effects or problems.

People have different attitudes about GM crops. In some countries, the law requires companies to say on the label if food contains GM crops.

Popular Choice

STORE GM

More than half of all foods sold in U.S. supermarkets are genetically modified. For example, GM soya is used to make all kinds of things from bread and cookies, to pizza and pasta. Cooking oil often contains GM rapeseed. In Europe, there is a different attitude toward GM crops and many stores have stopped using GM crops in food. There, all products containing more than 1 percent of GM food must have labels saying so.

WHAT ARE THE PROBLEMS?

GM foods are tested on animals such as fish, chickens, pigs, and rats. If the animals react badly then it is likely that humans will too. Some GM foods have had serious problems. GM potatoes have been tested on rats and pigs. The GM food harmed the internal organs of the rats. In another test, GM potatoes that had been modified with a gene to make bones grow faster were fed to pigs that later developed serious bone problems. GM potatoes could, in time, be better for you than nonGM potatoes. If scientists could successfully modify the vegetable so that it contains less starch, the potatoes would absorb less fat when fried, making them healthier.

NATURAL GM

GM happens naturally too. More than 1 billion people worldwide eat sweet potatoes. The sweet potato was the first food to be genetically modified—around 8,000 years ago! A bacterium inserted two of its genes into the original sweet potato DNA and a GM sweet potato was created.

CHAPTER 3

ALTERED ANIMALS

Nature has always produced some extraordinary looking creatures, but what happens when you experiment with genetics?

FLUORESCENT FISH

In the late 1990s, a group of scientists in China wanted to develop a fish that could detect pollution by becoming fluorescent when it swam through polluted water.

They hit upon a novel idea: use a gene from a jellyfish. Green fluorescent protein (GFP) is naturally fluorescent. The scientists inserted the gene into a zebra fish **embryo** so it became part of the fish's genome. As they hoped, the GFP caused the fish to be brightly colored and fluorescent under both natural light and ultraviolet light. When the fish was tested in polluted water, it turned green. The team experimented with other colors with genes from coral and other jellyfish. As a by-product of this research, a company in the United States developed the fish as novelty pets.

MODIFIED MICE

The United States and China are the world's leading centers of GM research on animals. In China, huge laboratories are experimenting on mice to discover the limits of GM. Researchers at Fudan University in Shanghai have genetically modified mice in more than 500 different ways to try to find cures to human diseases, like various cancers.

GM technology has enabled scientists to create animals with amazing new features, such as these GM GloFish.

A NATURAL BALANCE?

Every year, the World Health Organization (WHO) estimates that malaria infects 250 million people and kills half a million worldwide. In an attempt to control the disease, scientists are in the process of genetically modifying male mosquitoes so that they reproduce at a lower rate. The Sterile Insect Technique means that when a GM male mosquito mates with a wild female, its sperm can fertilize the female's eggs but the offspring die at an early stage of development. But what are the consequences of such a change? If thousands of sterile GM male mosquitoes were released into the environment, it could unbalance the ecosystem and cause a different pest to appear with a different disease.

Advances in biotechnology have led to the development of transgenic plants and animals. To create a transgenic plant or animal, pieces of DNA are taken from one organism and added to another.

The foreign genes are inserted into the genetic material of a single-cell embryo. When it grows into an adult, all the cells contain the new information, which might, for example, be a resistance to infectious disease. This is then passed on to future generations. However, critics of GM say that too many transgenic animals suffer horrible illnesses and health complications that lead to early death.

Designer livestock is at the cutting edge of GM research. If scientists can figure out ways of producing more food or improving the nutritional value of meat, public health could be improved. In China, researchers have created a GM cow that has beef that is rich in omega-3 fatty acids, which are commonly found in fish. There are also GM cows that produce milk like human breast milk, which could in turn replace formula milk.

SAFE SALMON?

In 2015, the U.S. Food and Drug Administration said that GM salmon is safe for humans to eat. This makes it the world's first GM animal to be eaten by humans. The salmon is grown in land tanks. There are very strict safety measures in place to prevent the fish escaping the tanks. The fish are also sterile so they cannot crossbreed with wild fish.

ECO-PIGS!

One of the most common sources of water pollution is a chemical called phosphorus. It causes algae to grow rapidly on the surface of ponds and lakes, which blocks sunlight and can kill fish and other organisms. Phosphorus is found in plants. When pigs and other animals eat plants, there is a lot of phosphorus in their manure, which can enter water sources. To minimize this, scientists in Canada genetically modified pig embryos with both mouse DNA and *E.coli* bacteria to make them produce less phosphorus.

For now, eco-pigs will only be raised in controlled research settings in Canada. They will go through years of safety trials before they can be approved for humans to eat.

A biotech company in China has produced miniature pigs, called micro-pigs. Customers will even be able to choose their desired color and coat pattern. It is already possible to genetically modify a dog, cat, or bird's size, enhance their intelligence, or correct genetic illnesses. Should we be worried about this fashion for customizing the DNA of our pets? Is it making light of the important science behind it? What are the outcomes for the animals?

DESIGNER DOGS

Domestic dogs have been selectively bred for hundreds of years. This means that humans have chosen certain desirable characteristics in one breed and mated it with another. If you want a gentle dog that is low allergy, very smart, and easy to train, you breed a poodle with a Labrador. The poodle's coat is **hypoallergenic** and the Labrador is smart. This crossbred dog is called a Labradoodle!

Many people think that selective breeding is a better option than GM because it is slower and seems more "natural." They worry that GM changes too much too fast and risks creating animals that suffer unpredictable problems. However, many dog breeds created in this way already suffer. Cavalier King Charles Spaniels have very small heads. They look pretty but some individuals have skulls that are too small for their brains so they are in terrible pain much of the time. Pugs have been bred to have flat faces but that makes it difficult for them to breathe properly. Sometimes, what we accept as the standard or even natural method of breeding is not any better than GM, and it is the animal that endures the consequences.

Almost all modern dog breeds have been bred or genetically modified for different reasons, such as appearance, tracking ability, and anti-allergy fur.

CUTTING EDGE

In October 2015, the first gene-edited dogs were reported to have been engineered in China. Scientists created a beagle with double the usual amount of muscle. They did this by deleting a gene called myostatin. The extra muscles improve the dogs' running ability. Beagles are very good tracker dogs so with better running ability, the new animals could have a future use for the police or the military.

CHAPTER 4

MAKING MEDICINE

One of the most exciting areas for the use of GM is in medicine. It also causes a lot of disagreement. Most people are happy for scientists to understand DNA and to know what genes are responsible for certain conditions but many people worry about where this knowledge could lead.

A number of advances have already been made based on our understanding of DNA, gene behavior, and our ability to isolate genes. GM is already reducing inherited diseases such as breast cancer. Women can have a test to find out whether they carry the faulty BRCA2 gene that causes the cancer and, if they do, they can opt to have surgery to prevent breast cancer from ever developing.

The actress Angelina Jolie carried the BRCA2 gene. In 2015, she elected to have surgery to minimize her chances of developing breast cancer.

One day, researchers will be able to treat a whole range of diseases that current medicines and medical techniques may not be able to. For example, cats suffer from a virus similar to HIV, which is a virus that causes serious illness in humans. Through genetically modifying cats, scientists are studying how the virus works in animals to help understand and treat the human virus better.

IMPROVING HUMAN WELFARE

A transgenic animal has had its genome changed to carry genes from another species. Transgenic mice, rabbits, pigs, sheep, goats, and cattle have all been created. Camels are next. Camels have been chosen because they are mostly disease-resistant. The transgenic camels produce GM milk that has curing proteins in it. This can then be processed to make medicines such as insulin to treat diabetes and clotting agents to treat hemophilia.

CUTTING EDGE

In the United States, goats have been genetically modified to produce human medicines. A chemical called ATryn is used to prevent blood clots in humans. Scientists have created a GM goat that produces ATryn in its milk. A segment of DNA was introduced into the goat's genes. This new DNA gave the goat a slightly altered genetic code.

GROWING ORGANS

Demand for new, healthy organs, such as kidneys and hearts, greatly outstrips supply. With the help of genetic modification, it might be possible to find a safe and plentiful supply of organs for transplant.

INTER-SPECIES ORGAN EXCHANGE

Xenotransplantation is the name for between-species organ transplants. So far, a pig heart has functioned in a baboon for 945 days and a kidney swap between these species lasted 136 days. The pigs were "humanized" with up to five human genes. This is done to limit the risk of rejection. These incredible advances could mean the difference between life and death for some human patients in the future.

FROM PIGS TO HUMANS?

Often, patients can wait for many months or even years before a suitable match is found, but genetic modification may be able to speed up the wait. In the future, pigs with livers, kidneys, and hearts suitable for transplantation into desperately sick people will be available. Researchers in the United States have modified the genes that have in the past meant the human body rejects the pig organ. They have also switched off more than 60 pig genes that carry viruses that could be passed on to the patient. In 2015, researchers in the United States reported that they will soon be ready to implant the GM embryos in mother pigs. The ability to safely transplant pig organs into humans could revolutionize transplant surgery and save people's lives.

There are thousands of people in the United States who are waiting for a heart transplant. Some wait for many years. GM could help reduce the waiting list and provide many more hearts.

GM RISKS

As with all experimental techniques, GM transplants must be trialed on a small number of humans before being given to the rest of the population. There are no long-term studies into the consequences of using GM organs from pigs or any other GM medicine. Is the risk worth taking? Do you think we should be told if our medicine is GM or not?

Gene therapy is one of the key areas of discussion and debate among scientists, political leaders, and the public, but what exactly is it? How does it work? How might it replace traditional medicine?

1. Gene therapy starts outside the human body and inside a laboratory. If a patient has an inherited disease, scientists can identify which gene is causing the illness.

2. The faulty gene is first isolated and then a new gene, without the fault, is created.

3. The new gene is put into a specially engineered virus.

4. Cells are removed from the patient and mixed with the virus.

5. The new cells are returned to the patient.

CHANGING INHERITANCE

If you are sick, you might see a doctor who will diagnose what is wrong and give you some medicine. Gene therapy could change how doctors work. It is possible that in the future, most of their work might be to prevent rather than cure illness. A future where gene therapy is widely adopted could mean that inherited genetic problems could be altered either in the uterus or in infancy to minimize the chances of becoming sick later in life.

FUTURE HOPE

Cystic fibrosis is a life-shortening, inherited disease. Symptoms include poor growth and excessive mucus, which causes breathing difficulties. It is estimated that more than 30,000 Americans have cystic fibrosis. The gene that causes the condition was identified more than 25 years ago. Scientists believe there might be a treatment within the next five years. Researchers in the United Kingdom have developed a technique to enable patients to breathe in molecules of DNA, which deliver a normal copy of the faulty gene to cells in the lung.

CUTTING EDGE

In 2015, doctors in London, England, successfully treated a one-year-old child who had "incurable" leukemia. They had already tried chemotherapy and a bone marrow transplant. The doctors treated her with a genetic therapy that used designer **immune cells**. In total, the child was given 50 million GM cells that would hunt and kill the cancer. The disease vanished, and she is now a fully healthy child.

CHAPTER 5

CLONING

A clone is an exact copy. In biology, this means that a multicellular, or many-celled, organism is genetically identical to another living organism. The word "clone" was first used in 1963 by British geneticist J.B.S. Haldane (1892–1964).

Cloning and genetic modification are not the same, but cloning techniques are used in genetic engineering. Genetic engineering produces a unique set of genes that can then be swapped across species to genetically modify them. Cloning, however, produces exact copies of genes and these are copied within the same species. Cloning an organism means to create a new organism with the exact same genetic information as the existing one. This can be done by a process called somatic cell nuclear transfer.

Identical twins are like clones because they have the same DNA. However, they are not clones because they have different fingerprints.

CUTTING EDGE

Crossing over genes from animals into humans and vice versa is one of the most sensitive areas of genetic research. In many countries, scientists have already created animal-**hybrid** embryos in laboratories. It is not known whether some of these embryos have developed into actual creatures.

This means that the central portion, the nucleus, is removed from an egg cell and replaced with a nucleus taken from a cell of the organism to be cloned. As the nucleus contains all the genetic information of a life-form, the host egg cell will develop into an organism genetically identical to the nucleus donor. Mice, frogs, and cattle have been cloned in this way.

A SPECIAL SHEEP

In 1996, a very special animal was born at the University of Edinburgh in Scotland. Dolly the sheep was the first mammal to be cloned using an adult animal. Her creation was considered a huge success and a giant leap forward for genetics research. However, the success rate for cloning is very low. Dolly was born after nearly 300 failed attempts. Fewer than 100 calves have been created from more than 9,000 attempts, and many of them have died young. Some species, such as horses and dogs, have yet to be successfully cloned at all. Dolly herself lived for seven years, about half the average lifespan for a sheep.

It may seem like a story straight out of a science fiction movie, but GM humans may be a reality in the near future. Some scientists believe the first humans who have had their DNA genetically modified could exist within a few years. But there are issues surrounding the use of this biotechnology, for individuals and for any future offspring who would have an altered genetic code passed on to them.

GENE-EDITING TECHNOLOGY

Snipping away parts of a person's DNA is what is known as gene-editing. It is a process that can be used to correct faulty genes. Some people suffer from a genetic condition called leber congenital amaurosis. This is a condition in which a faulty gene stops the creation of a protein in the **retina**. The protein is essential for vision. Eventually, sufferers can lose their sight. Scientists in the United States want to trial gene-editing on blind patients. If permission is given, the patients' eyes would be injected with special viruses. These would be coded to delete part of the patients' DNA and correct the gene.

SUPER SOLDIERS?

In the United States, the Defense Advanced Research Projects Agency is exploring whether, by manipulating genes, tomorrow's soldiers could carry heavier weights or go for longer without food or sleep. They are even exploring whether it would be possible to regrow limbs that have been lost in battle.

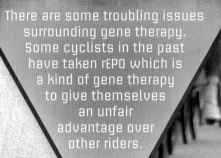

There are some troubling issues surrounding gene therapy. Some cyclists in the past have taken rEPO which is a kind of gene therapy to give themselves an unfair advantage over other riders.

HUMAN CLONES?

Using genetic knowledge and applying it to human DNA, it is technically possible for scientists to clone a human. Many people believe that trying to clone a human being would be morally wrong and should not be attempted. However, some scientists have stated that it is the final frontier of genetic research and they are going to try it. Given that animal cloning success rates are very low, it seems a distant prospect. It is possible that someone somewhere is working on it right now, but for many, this crosses a moral line.

DESIGNER BABIES

The idea of designing your room, your clothes, or even a home is appealing to many people, but what about designing a human being? The science is not there yet, but in the future, people might be able to do just this.

RIGHT OR WRONG?

Regardless of their own genetic makeup, should parents be able to request a blonde-haired, blue-eyed baby or a dark-haired, olive-skinned baby? Gene-editing is a process that many worry will lead to a demand for what are known as designer babies. Critics say that the outcome for a baby born from technology like gene-editing is unknown. Another concern is that this process could damage the **gene pool**. Certain genes might become fashionable in one generation and then become harmful to the next.

MORE THAN TWO PARENTS

In 2001, it emerged that the world's first genetically modified human babies had been born in the United States. The children were born to women who had difficulties in conceiving. Genetic fingerprint tests on the children showed that they had DNA from more than three "parents." Should the children one day have their own children, this DNA will be passed on to them. While some people hailed the achievement as a scientific breakthrough, many people were horrified at the tampering with the genetic makeup of our species.

CUTTING EDGE

Every year, almost 8 million children are born with serious birth defects. Mostly, these defects are genetically caused. If genetic errors were corrected using biotechnology and gene therapy in the uterus when the child is an embryo, it would get rid of these defects and diseases. Gene-editing could limit the death rates of people with inherited conditions as well as those with heart disease, cancer, and diabetes.

Gene-editing could be used to give everyone the chance to live healthily into old age.

Ethics means the moral principles that govern a person's behavior and make us decide what we think is right and what we think is wrong. The debate surrounding genetic modification, its acceptable uses, and its potential is called bioethics. It is a truly global issue, and opinions are swayed by culture and politics as well as by religious beliefs.

YOU DECIDE

Some people view all genetic modification with distrust. They believe that we should not tamper with nature. However, other people think that this new science could hold the key to getting rid of diseases and harnessing unlimited animal and plant resources to feed the world. Think about your own opinion and where you stand in the debate. Where are you going to draw your own ethical line?

THE CASE FOR . . .

As genetics allows us to reduce human disease, it is also granting us the power to engineer desirable characteristics in humans. With GM, we could create a breed of superstrong people to be a labor force or supersmart people to use science and technology to solve global problems. We could also, potentially, through GM, enable people to live longer.

. . . AND THE CASE AGAINST

The main concern with any new science is safety. Most scientists around the world agree to ethical standards, which mean that no experiments should be conducted where there is a risk of harm to the participant. A lot of people worry about tampering with nature. Opponents of GM argue that just because you can do something, it does not mean it is right.

Would it be right to create GM humans capable of extraordinary speed or other abilities, or should traits like this only arise naturally and through hard work and dedicated training?

BEYOND CONTROL?

At present, there is no global body to oversee the development or the ethical use of genetic biotechnology. Each country monitors its own scientists. Is this sufficient? While many people want to embrace the new possibilities of GM and see how far it can go, there are at least an equal number who are concerned about uncontrolled, unethical practices.

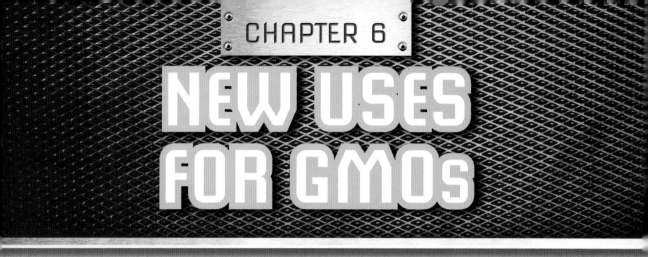

CHAPTER 6

NEW USES FOR GMOs

In the world of GM, exciting scientific breakthroughs happen all the time. These successes suggest a bright future and a better quality of life for many. From revolutionary cell treatments to pollution-fighting plants, GM could give real hope to very sick people and help our environment, too.

WONDER CELLS

Stem cells are special because they have properties that no other cells have: they can perform many different functions in the body. Stem cells change to form muscle, nerve, skin, and even organ cells. Scientists hope to take stem cells from the blood in **umbilical cords** and use them to modify faulty genes and repair damaged organs. They also think that stem cells could repair damage to nerves in the spinal column. This would enable paralyzed people to walk again.

CUTTING EDGE

It is now possible to target specific parts of an organism's DNA. This means that scientists can isolate, or separate, genes and cut them out if they are faulty. This is done with a chemical **enzyme**. The enzyme is helped by a guide molecule. Together, they are called molecular scissors because they snip away at the unwanted part of the genome. This is how gene therapy works for some leukemia treatments.

GROUNDBREAKING ADVANCES IN GM

Transgenic plants that can clean up contamination sites by absorbing polluted groundwater through their roots are giving scientists hope for reducing environmental pollution. A biotech company in the United States wants to use poplar trees to clear up the site of a former oil storage facility in Indiana. In laboratory tests, the GM plants absorbed more than 30 times as much pollution as wild plants.

Spider silk is about five times stronger than steel of the same diameter. It could be used to make all sorts of things including artificial ligaments, but up until now it has not been possible to produce it on the huge scale that would be required. Researchers have inserted a silk gene from a spider into a goat's DNA and coded it so that the goat produces silk in its milk. This "silk milk" could then be used to make a very strong, very flexible weblike material.

Bioscience is allowing researchers to look at and access the natural world in new and exciting ways. Most medicines come from plants, and scientists now want to explore and exploit plant properties at a genetic level. One of the most advanced uses of this biotechnology is in the production of GM crops to make medicine.

Pharmacrops are genetically modified to produce pharmaceuticals, or medical drugs. In the United States, the California Rice Commission wants to grow almost 124 acres (50 hectares) of GM rice near San Diego. In laboratory conditions, two types of GM rice are being grown. They have been modified with synthetic, or artificially made, human genes. The first plant has been modified to make human lactoferrin, which is used to treat the blood disease anemia. The second plant produces a chemical called lysozyme, which is used to treat diarrhea. These are two serious conditions, particularly in parts of the world where there are food shortages or even famine. They can become killers. There is a lot of public concern and so far, permission has not been granted to bring the plants out of the laboratory.

CUTTING EDGE

A U.S. company is developing an anthrax vaccine. Anthrax is a deadly disease spread by bacteria that could also be used as a devastating **biological weapon**. By the transgenic genetic engineering of the petunia flower, the flower can be made to manufacture new proteins which, when eaten, prompt the development of anti-anthrax **antibodies**. This would make a person immune to the disease.

Bioscience could help create vaccines and make us safe from dangerous bacteria, such as *Bacillus anthracis* [shown here], which causes anthrax.

NATURE IN THE BALANCE?

As with GM crops in general, there are real concerns about the safety of pharmacrops. Pesticides are sprayed on all crops. We know that some of the pesticides sink into the soil and enter the water cycle. When insects eat the crop, they absorb these harmful chemicals. When they, in turn, are eaten by larger animals, the poison is passed on. In the same way, birds and other animals could pass on harmful effects of GM crops. Bees could also spread GM pollen.

Cows, pigs, sheep, and chickens are all experimented on using various GM techniques to fight human diseases and to help the environment. From genetically modifying cows that produce less methane, a type of gas, to limit global warming, to sheep that produce double the amount of both milk and wool, biotechnology seems to offer many possibilities.

Researchers at Edinburgh University, in Scotland, are developing a pig that is "edited" with a warthog gene. They are hoping that the GM pig will be able to resist African swine fever, a disease that has no vaccine and has resulted in the widespread slaughter of pigs across eastern Europe. If the tests go well and legal permission is given, the GM pig could be ready for sale within a decade.

Warthogs have a natural, chemical immunity to a deadly pig disease. By using this gene and putting it into other pigs, researchers are hopeful that the pigs will be immune too.

LACTO-FREE!

Millions of people all over the world are lactose intolerant. This means that they do not produce an enzyme in their gut called lactase so they cannot digest the lactose in milk. In New Zealand, researchers have genetically modified a cow that produces lactose-free milk. They created the cow by taking a cow skin cell and using GM to produce molecules that block the lactose protein. The nucleus of this cell was then put into a cow egg that had its own nucleus removed. The egg was developed in the lab before being moved into the uterus of a host cow.

In Seoul, South Korea, researchers have developed a "double-muscled" pig. By editing a single gene, these pigs have leaner meat and a higher yield of meat per animal. These pigs are being aimed at the Chinese market where demand for pork is increasing.

So far, few of these animals have left the laboratory. Some people feel that it is dangerous to tamper with nature while others are excited by the potential for enhancing human life. What do you think?

GENETIC MODIFICATION POTENTIAL

GM science is only about 30 years old and new ways of using it are being figured out all the time. However, exactly what the future holds for GMOs could be dependent on our attitudes to them.

As with any new science, there are positives and negatives to the technology. Improved productivity from GM crops could result in producing more food from less land and feeding more people. GM pest- and disease-resistant crops could reduce the need for pesticides and other chemicals, so fewer toxins would be present to harm the environment. GM could be used to make healthier food, by eliminating unhealthy fats or caffeine, for example. GM could also be used to remove genes associated with allergies, for example, blocking the gene that produces the allergenic protein in peanuts.

CUTTING EDGE

In 2015, scientists in China created the first GM human embryo. Some scientists argue that studying GM embryos could mean preventing children being born with cystic fibrosis or genes that increase the risk of cancer. Others say that the long-term outcomes of GM embryos are completely unknown. They also say that it is morally wrong to create life only for experimentation. What do you think?

In the future, GM could enable more crops to be grown in drought-affected regions of the world, increasing food available for the global population.

TOMORROW'S SCIENCE TODAY

In the future, GM could change how long and how well people live. It may mean that some children have more than two biological parents. GMOs are not just part of a science fiction fantasy future but part of our present-day scientific fact. And the sooner that scientists, leaders, and people understand its potential, safe use, and control, the sooner GMOs and genetic modifications can begin to be of benefit to everyone.

GLOSSARY

antibodies substances produced by cells in the body that counteract the effects of germs

bacteria tiny organisms made up of only one cell

biological weapon a weapon that uses "natural" poisons to cause death or disease on a large scale

biotechnology the use of biology, including genetics, for industrial and other purposes

chromosomes strings of DNA found in the cell nucleus

deoxyribonucleic acid (DNA) a chemical substance that carries each person's genetic information

embryo an unborn and developing human or animal

enzyme a substance in plants and animals that can speed up chemical reactions

gene pool the total collection of genes in a population

genes codes formed from DNA that govern how living things develop

genetic code the order of the chemicals in DNA

hybrid the offspring of two different plants or animals

hypoallergenic nonallergic

immune cells special cells that protect against germs and disease

molecule the smallest unit of a substance, made up of atoms

nucleus the control center of a cell that contains the chromosomes

retina the part of the eye that receives images

umbilical cords feeding tubes that connect fetuses with their mothers during pregnancy

FOR MORE INFORMATION

BOOKS

Hartman, Eve. *What are the Issues with Genetic Technology?* (Sci-Hi: Science Issues). North Mankato, MN: Raintree, 2012.

Mooney, Carla. *Genetics: Breaking the Code of Your DNA.* (Inquire and Investigate). White River Junction, VT: Nomad Press, 2014.

Petersen, Christine. *Genetics* (The Science of Life). Edina, MN: Abdo Publishing Company, 2014.

WEBSITES

Find out more information about what genes are and how gene therapy works at:
kidshealth.org/kid/talk/qa/what_is_gene.html

Visit this website for a full overview of the issues surrounding GMOs:
www.kidsrighttoknow.com/gmos

Read this page to learn more about cells, then click "In the cell" for many more related articles:
www.yourgenome.org/facts/what-is-a-cell

INDEX

bacteria 6, 7, 15, 17, 21, 40
biotechnology 4, 20, 32, 35, 37, 40, 42
breeding 10, 12, 20, 22, 36

cancers 18, 24, 29, 35, 44
cells 6, 8, 20, 28, 29, 30, 31, 38, 43
cloning 30–31, 33
cotton 10
Crick, Francis 9
crops 4, 10–11, 15, 16, 17, 40–41, 44
cystic fibrosis 29, 44

Darwin, Charles 8
diabetes 9, 25, 35
diseases 4, 5, 8, 10, 18, 19, 20, 24, 25, 28, 29, 35, 36, 40, 42, 44
dogs 22, 23, 31
Dolly 31

enzymes 38, 43
ethics 33, 34, 36, 37

farming 4, 10, 11, 12, 16
fish 4, 5, 12, 17, 18, 20, 21
fluorescence 18
food 4, 9, 10, 11, 12, 14–15, 16–17, 20, 32, 40, 44

gene-editing 23, 32, 34, 35, 42, 43
genes 4, 5, 6, 7, 9, 11, 12, 13, 15, 17, 18, 20, 23, 24, 25, 26, 28, 29, 30, 31, 32, 34, 38, 39, 40, 42, 43, 44
gene therapy 28–29, 35, 38
genetic code 4, 25, 32
genomes 9, 18, 25, 38
goats 25, 39

Haldane, J.B.S. 30

inheritance 6, 7, 8, 24, 28, 29, 35

medicine 4, 9, 24–25, 27, 28, 29, 40
Mendel, Gregor 6, 8
Miescher, Friedrich 8

pharmacrops 40–41
pigs 12, 13, 17, 21, 22, 25, 26, 27, 42, 43
pollution 11, 18, 21, 38, 39

selective breeding 10, 12, 22
Sturtevant, Alfred 9

Tijo, Joe Hin 9
transgenics 20–21, 25, 39, 40
transplants 26, 29

Watson, James 9